P9-CEZ-755

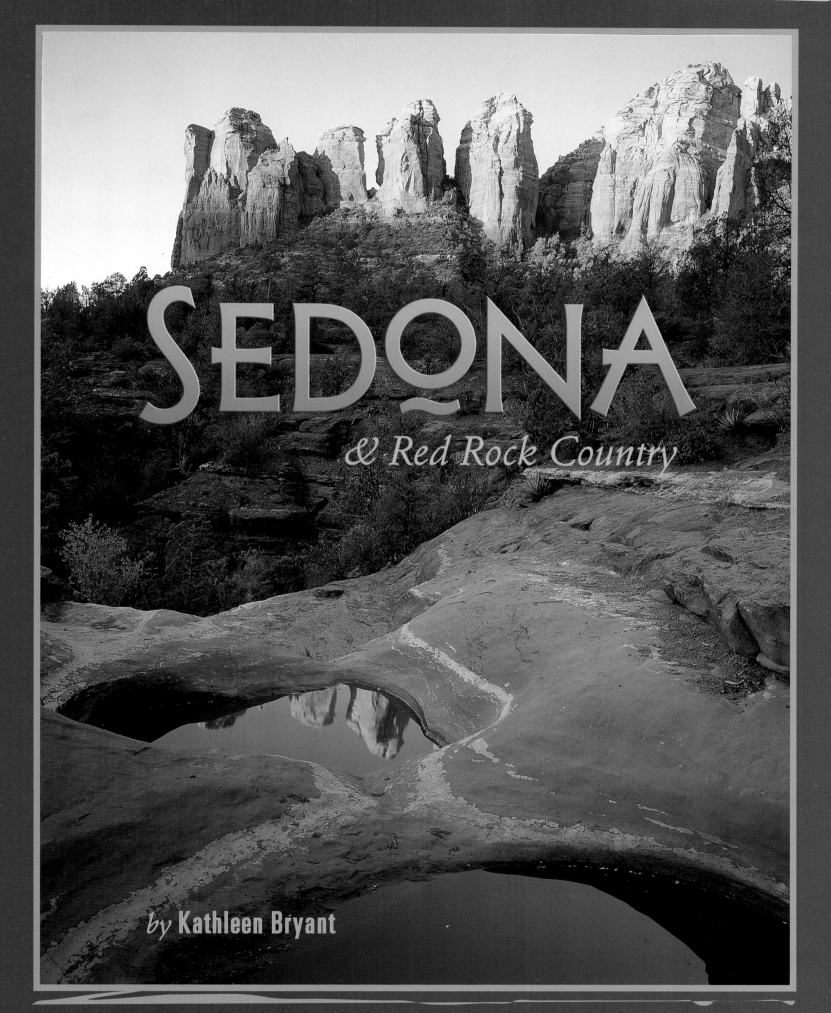

SEDONA
& Red Rock Country

by **Kathleen Bryant**

RIO NUEVO
PUBLISHERS

CONTENTS

Above: Agaves.
Right: New Age medicine wheel.

RED ROCK COUNTRY

A two hour's drive north of Phoenix,
Sedona's Red Rock Country is neither
desert nor mountain but a landscape
in-between, encompassing five hundred
square miles of colorful buttes and
canyons carved from the southern edge
of the Colorado Plateau. The vast upland
extending around the Four Corners of the
Southwest is called the Mogollon
(locally pronounced "muggy-own") Rim.
The rim slices through central Arizona,
creating the escarpments bordering
Sedona to the north and east. Mingus
Mountain, across the Verde Valley, marks
the western horizon.

Snoopy Rock at twlight.
Inset: The Nuns.
Above right: View of Capitol Butte
and Coffeepot Rock from airport.

Red Rock Panoramas

Each of Sedona's three populated areas—Uptown, West Sedona, and the Village of Oak Creek—boasts astonishing views that are easy to appreciate on foot or from your car.

Uptown

The highest peak in Sedona, 7,122-foot-tall Wilson Mountain, towers over Uptown's shops and galleries. Below Wilson are sail-shaped Ship Rock and the long red deck of Steamboat. To the east, Teapot Rock and the Giant's Thumb contrast against the juniper-covered slopes of Schnebly Hill. Snoopy reclines near the buff-and-orange striped ridge known as Camel Head. The buttressed cliffs on the eastern horizon are peaked by Munds and Lee Mountains.

West Sedona

For the finest West Sedona views, drive up Airport Mesa to the popular vista at the top. Capitol Butte, the dome-shaped mountain to the north, dominates the 180-degree panorama. Formations rising above the residential areas of West Sedona include (west to east) Chimney Rock, Lizard Head (looking out from the side of Capitol Butte), and Sugarloaf.

The Boynton Canyon area, visible to the northwest, is marked by flat-topped Doe Mesa and Bear Mountain. East of Capitol Butte, the Sphinx guards Soldier's Pass.

Village of Oak Creek

Terrific views stretch along the Red Rock Scenic Byway, eight miles of State Route 179 between Uptown and the Village of Oak Creek. Elephant Rock trumpets above the highway near Broken Arrow. At the Chapel of the Holy Cross, you'll get an up-close look at the Nuns and the Madonna, plus a stunning vista that includes Bell Rock and Courthouse Butte to the south and Cathedral Rock to the west.

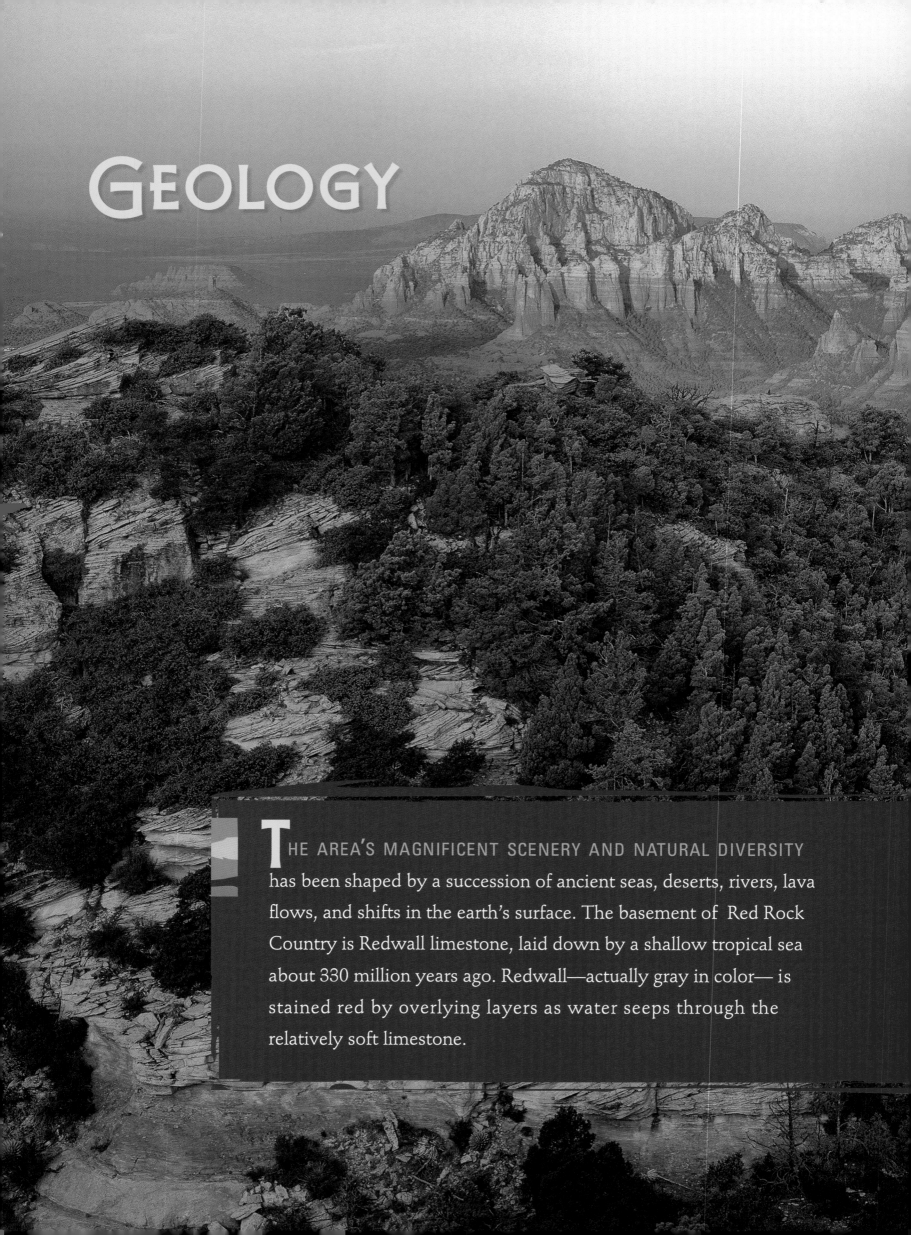

GEOLOGY

THE AREA'S MAGNIFICENT SCENERY AND NATURAL DIVERSITY has been shaped by a succession of ancient seas, deserts, rivers, lava flows, and shifts in the earth's surface. The basement of Red Rock Country is Redwall limestone, laid down by a shallow tropical sea about 330 million years ago. Redwall—actually gray in color— is stained red by overlying layers as water seeps through the relatively soft limestone.

Courthouse Rock, Cathedral Rock, Munds
Mountain, and the Mogollon Rim

Between 285 and 275 million years ago, river channels carried debris from an ancient mountain range near the present-day Rockies, creating a large delta. The resulting mudstone, sandstone, and conglomerate make up the Hermit formation. Most of Sedona's building sites and roads are cut into this layer's dark red, shaley surface.

Rising above are cliffs, buttes, and spires carved from the Schnebly Hill Formation, a seven-hundred-foot thick series of mudstone, sandstone, and limestone layers. Once coastal sand dunes, these richly colored rocks have been shaped by water and wind into fantastical forms: a mermaid, a coffeepot, a cartoon character. A thin, oxidized iron deposit coats individual grains of sand within the stone, coloring it rusty red.

When the limestone dissolves and the layers above collapse, sinkholes can form, such as Devil's Dining Room (found along the Broken Arrow Trail) and Devil's Kitchen (near Soldiers Pass).

Overlying the Redwall are four reddish layers about six hundred feet thick, known collectively as the Supai group. They formed 320 to 285 million years ago when the Sedona area was a coastal plain between two seas that rose and fell, leaving alternating strata of sandstone and mudstone. Supai rocks are exposed in Wilson Canyon, beneath Midgley Bridge north of Uptown Sedona, and along Beaver Creek, south of Sedona.

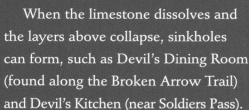

Left: Coffeepot Rock is shrouded in morning fog.
Above: The red rock cliffs of Boynton Canyon.

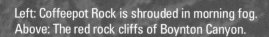

Above: Sandstone spire in Secret Canyon.
Right: Lee Mountain and other peaks in Munds Mountain Wilderness.

Running through the reddish layers is a ten- to twelve-foot grayish band of Fort Apache limestone. Near Boynton Canyon, the limestone thins out, marking the edge of an ancient sea. Here and there, the harder limestone forms an erosion-resistant cap that protects lower, softer rock, like the chunk of Fort Apache that forms Snoopy's nose.

Above the reddish cliffs is buff-colored Coconino sandstone, angled stacks formed from ancient windblown dunes. Because dunes formed continuously as the coastline shifted about 270 to 265 million years ago, Coconino sandstone merges in places with the Schnebly Hill strata below, leaving a landscape striped and blended in marvelous hues.

Left: A storm approaches Mitten Ridge. Above: Oak Creek's West Fork.

From 265 to 262 million years ago, another shallow sea advanced toward the desert, forming a three-hundred-foot-thick layer of sandstone that changes to gypsum northwest of Sedona. Some geologists consider this a continuation of the Coconino sandstone, which it resembles, while others refer to it as the Toroweap formation. On higher peaks, the Toroweap formation rises above a green band of vegetation and appears somewhat paler than the wind-deposited layers below.

The buttressed wall of cliffs forming Sedona's eastern horizon mark a rugged peninsula separated from the Colorado Plateau by Jacks Canyon. The highest points, Lee and Munds mountains, are topped by the Kaibab formation, fossil-bearing limestone laid down 260 to 255 million years ago by a vast sea. The Kaibab formation shapes the Mogollon Rim, as well as the rim of the Grand Canyon.

Throughout eras of time, continents shifted, creating mountain ranges and rivers that carried away and deposited debris. Lava flows from a volcanic period beginning about 15 million years ago formed basalt escarpments and outcroppings. A fault line, the precursor of Oak Creek Canyon, filled with successive lava flows that were then carved out by gravelly runoff. A mere 6 to 8 million years ago, a volcanic eruption crowned Wilson Mountain with basalt.

Sedona's magnificent landscape may appear to be frozen in time, but geologic forces continue to shape the land. Sandstone sometimes fissures and sloughs off to form corners, chimneys, and even arches like Devil's Bridge. According to geologists, Sedona's cliffs recede to the north at an average rate of about twelve inches every six hundred years.

Climb the mountains and get their good tidings.
Nature's peace will flow into you as sunshine flows
into trees. The winds will blow their own freshness
into you, and the storms their energy, while cares
will drop off like autumn leaves. —JOHN MUIR

Top: Vista from Schnebly Hill.
Left: Autumn oak leaves in Oak Creek.

NATURAL HISTORY

WITH ELEVATIONS FROM 3,500 TO 7,000 FEET, the Sedona area lies in a transition zone between the high Colorado Plateau of northeastern Arizona and the basin and range country to the south. Orientation to the sun, rainfall amounts (ten inches greater in Oak Creek Canyon than Sedona), and differences in terrain and soils create a range of microclimates within eight different biological communities.

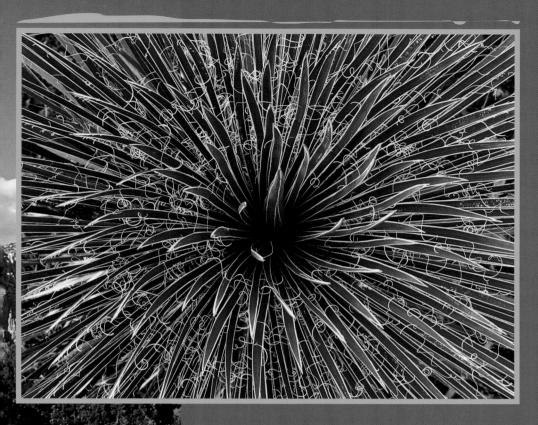

Above: Yucca leaves create a whorled design.
Left: Lewisia amid pine needles on the Mogollon Rim.
Opposite: Owl's clover blooms below Courthouse Rock.
Overleaf: Agave on the rim of Schnebly Hill, with the sun setting behind Wilson Mountain.

The predominant biological community in the Sedona area is piñon-juniper woodland, nicknamed "PJ." Its small trees include piñon, Utah juniper, and most common, one-seed juniper. This round-shaped juniper is dioecious, meaning some trees are male and some are female. Female trees yield cones that look like bluish berries. Male trees bear inconspicuous flowers, most noticeable as golden pollen in late winter and early spring—the bane of locals who sneeze and sniffle their way through "juniper season."

Desert grassland predominates near the Village of Oak Creek. Here, soaptree yucca, crucifixion thorn, grama grass, and prickly pear cactus provide food and shelter for lizards, snakes, and roadrunners. Pine-fir forest tops Wilson Mountain and shades north-facing canyon slopes. Northwest of Sedona, steep, shaley canyons hide mini-forests of Arizona cypress, as well as oak woodlands with Emory and Gambel oaks, netleaf hackberry, hoptree, and buckthorn.

But plants and animals aren't aware of the neat scientific boundaries assigned to them. Prickly pear cactus and rattlesnakes are commonly seen in piñon-juniper woodlands that border desert grasslands, and chaparral species—manzanita, catclaw acacia, and scrub oak—can be found on most south-facing slopes. This intermixture of neighboring communities is referred to as an ecotone, where flora and fauna mingle in amazing variety—over 500 types of plants; 55 mammals; 180 birds; some 35 snakes, lizards, and amphibians; 20 or more fishes; and thousands of insects and invertebrates.

Left: A rare heavy snow blanketed Sedona in white.
Top: Bigtooth maples drop their red leaves in fall.
Above: Great blue herons can be spotted along Oak Creek.

The spring-fed waters of Oak Creek create lush upper and lower riparian environments, where golden columbines tangle with blackberry canes beneath the spreading branches of Arizona sycamores. Native roundtail chub and speckled dace swim with introduced species like rainbow trout. The creek is also home to numerous amphibians, such as canyon tree frogs, tiger salamanders, and Woodhouse's toads. Great blue herons, egrets, mergansers, mallards, and flycatchers are a few of the birds that prefer creek-side habitat. Campers in Oak Creek Canyon might spot tassel-eared Abert's squirrels and nocturnal mammals like skunks, raccoons, and ringtails.

Below: Black-chinned hummingbirds and an Abert's squirrel.

Right: Oak Creek's West Fork mirrors the trees and rocks above.

Oak Creek, Beaver Creek, and the Verde River are the region's only permanent sources of surface water, but rainstorms and snowmelt can turn dry washes into ephemeral streams or create waterfalls that briefly spout from canyon walls. Deep erosion-carved bedrock pools hold water into the dry foresummer, though in particularly dry years, shy canyon denizens such as black bear and mountain lions may wander into town to quench their thirst.

Sedona is a birder's paradise, home to an array of species from tiny black-chinned hummingbirds to majestic bald eagles. Rocky canyons echo with the piercing cries of falcons and other raptors. Roadrunners race through desert grasslands, while acorn woodpeckers and goshawks prefer the secrecy of canyon forests. Ravens—the bad boys of the bird world—chortle to each other from parking lot lampposts and hang around local restaurants, waiting to steal away with a tasty morsel. Many species nest here during summer, wintering in Mexico or Central and South America. Seventeen are on the Threatened and Endangered Species list, including the peregrine falcon and the common black hawk.

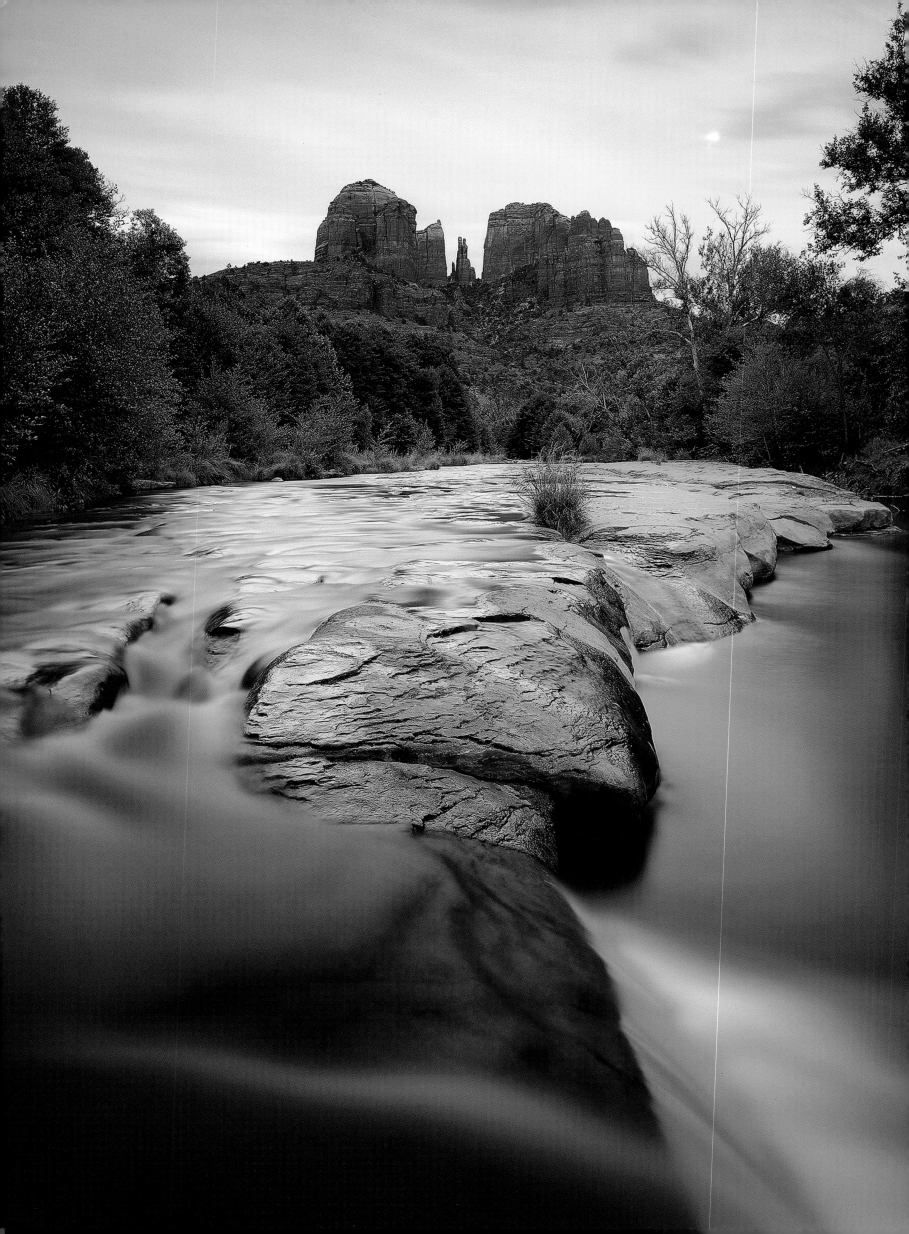

Some ten thousand insect species fly, wriggle, and crawl through the Southwestern deserts, and Sedona has its share. Students at the local high school chose the venomous scorpion for their school mascot. Tarantulas, the gentle giants of the insect world, wander across streets and roads during monsoon season in search of mates. Centipedes and water striders are depicted in centuries-old rock art galleries.

Lizards, snakes, and other reptiles are ectotherms, unable to regulate their body temperature internally. During warmer months, you're likely to see whiptail lizards darting across a trail or fence lizards climbing a stucco wall. Rattlesnake sightings are less common, though several species—Arizona black, black-tailed, Western

diamondback, and Mohave rattlers—call the Sedona area home. Rattlers are most active at snake-friendly temperatures around 80 degrees F. This means shade or twilight in summer months, so be especially careful hiking after sunset.

Nearly every night, coyotes serenade the town, and though you may never catch sight of the piglike collared peccary, better known as a javelina, hike nearly any trail and you'll spot its hoofprints, similar to deer tracks but smaller and closer together. Though Red Rock Country might seem dry and rocky on a hot summer afternoon, life here is diverse and abundant.

Above (clockwise from left): Javelina mother and baby, coyotes, and a western diamondback rattlesnake all inhabit the area around Sedona.

Opposite: The full moon rises behind thin cirrus clouds over Cathedral Rock at Red Rock Crossing.

SEASONS *of* SEDONA

Locals sometimes joke that Sedona has only two seasons—December and tourist season. But the elevation, topography, and rich plant life combine to create something rare in Arizona, four distinct seasons with golden autumn leaves, winter snows, spring wildflowers, and yes, sizzling summers.

The moderate semi-arid climate draws šnowbirdš who seek relief from northern winters and summer visitors who flee the desert for cool high-country evenings. In winter, daytime temperatures rarely drop below forty degrees, and even on the hottest July day, when afternoon temperatures can top one hundred, mornings and evenings are comfortable.

Sedona has two rainy seasons. Gentle winter showers can linger two or three days, sometimes with overnight snow melting by afternoon from all but the highest peaks. Though frosts and heavy snows are possible into April, signs of spring—wildflowers and apricot blossoms—may appear as early as February. As May approaches, daytime temperatures begin to climb toward the nineties, and the sky turns cloudless blue.

Weeks may pass without rain, leaving the forest vulnerable to wildfire. (The human-caused Brins Fire of 2006 burned more than four thousand acres.) Summer rains bring relief by mid-July, typically in the form of brief, localized afternoon thunderstorms. Most of Sedona's annual precipitation of seventeen inches falls during this monsoon period, which usually lasts until mid-September.

Left: Autumn in Oak Creek.
Above: The Dude Fire burns on the Mogollon Rim near Sedona.

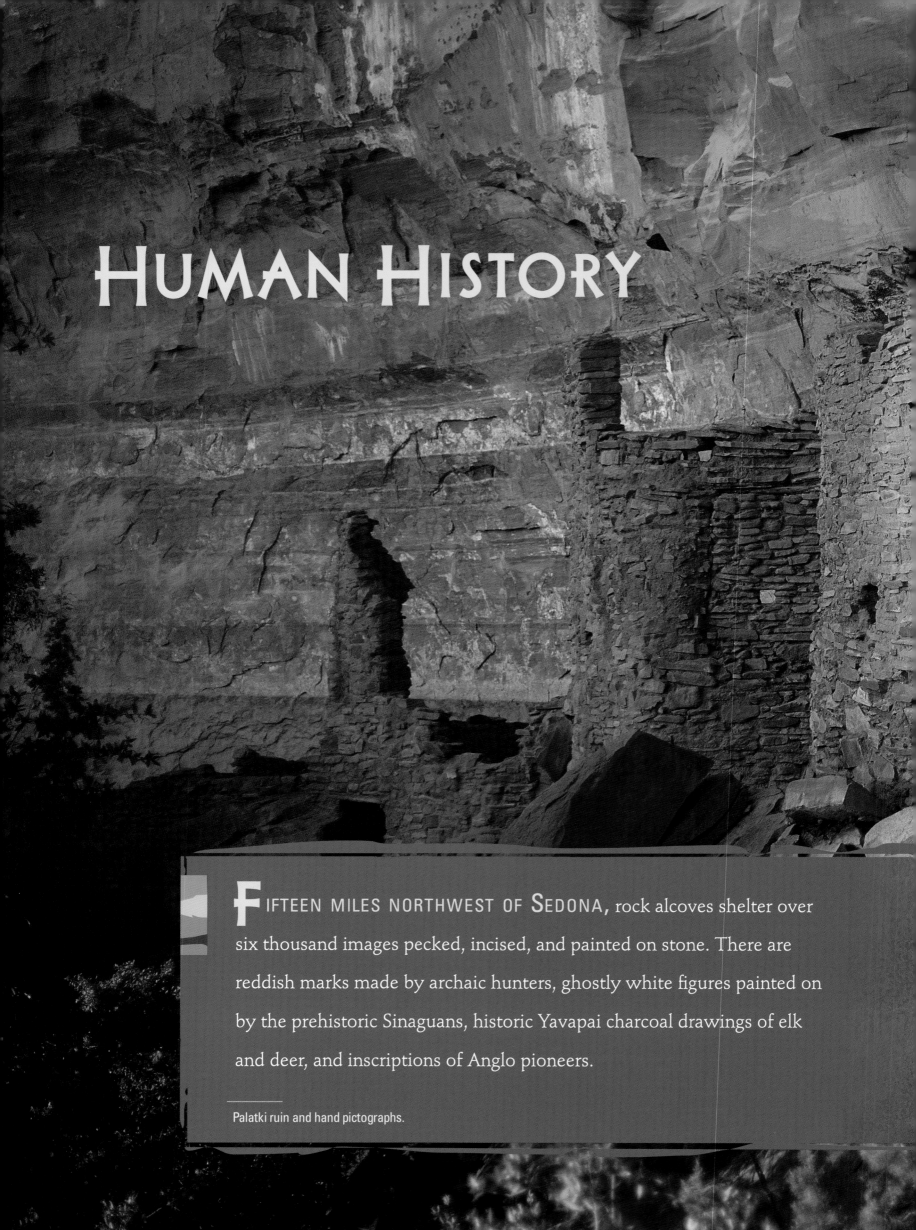

HUMAN HISTORY

FIFTEEN MILES NORTHWEST OF SEDONA, rock alcoves shelter over six thousand images pecked, incised, and painted on stone. There are reddish marks made by archaic hunters, ghostly white figures painted on by the prehistoric Sinaguans, historic Yavapai charcoal drawings of elk and deer, and inscriptions of Anglo pioneers.

Palatki ruin and hand pictographs.

The Old Ones

Clovis points found nearby suggest that Paleo-Indians roamed through Red Rock Country in search of game more than eight thousand years ago. Hunters hafted these long stone points to thrusting spears or darts and used them to bring down large Pleistocene mammals. Because people depended upon the environment for food, shelter, and clothing, technological advances were linked to the landscape. As the climate grew warmer and drier, megafauna became extinct. Hunters sought smaller game, such as deer, and began to make smaller points for atlatls, or throwing spears. Archaic hunter-gatherers traveled from one area to the next as seasons changed and different plants matured.

The most dramatic shift came when people began to plant and tend crops, requiring year-round dwellings rather than temporary camps. The prehistoric Southwest farmers who built homes and villages out of stone are referred to as Ancestral Puebloans. The Ancestral Puebloan culture is made up of many small regional populations, including the Sinaguas, whose territories centered around the San Francisco Peaks.

Above: Sinagua ruin in Loy Canyon.
Right: Lichens and Sinagua petroglyphs of perhaps a bobcat with other figures.

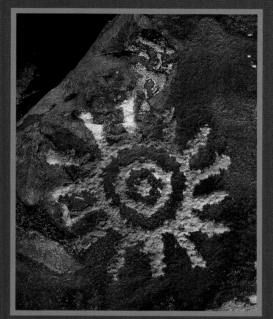

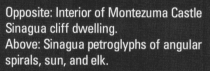
Opposite: Interior of Montezuma Castle Sinagua cliff dwelling.
Above: Sinagua petroglyphs of angular spirals, sun, and elk.

The Sinaguas

Farming began relatively late in the Sedona area, around A.D. 650, probably because of the abundant resources this area offered gatherers. People continued to use agave, yucca, walnuts, piñon nuts, berries, plantain, and other wild foods even after they became farmers. Pottery came into use for cooking and storage, and still smaller points were knapped for arrows and bows.

These prehistoric farmers constructed pit houses—large, partly underground rooms—and lived in small hamlets. Beginning around A.D. 1100, they began building pueblos (villages of contiguous rooms) in red rock canyons. They preferred south-facing dwellings, shaded in summer and warmed by the winter sun's rays, protected from rain and snow by the cliffs above.

The first to name this group of Ancestral Puebloans, whose territory extended from the San Francisco Peaks south to the Verde Valley, was Harold Colton, founder of Flagstaff's Museum of Northern Arizona. He called them Sinagua, from the old Spanish name for the Peaks, the Sierra Sin Agua (Mountains Without Water). But long before Colton "discovered" the Sinaguas, locals knew about their ruined villages.

Jesse Walter Fewkes, the first to study the cliff dwellings of Red Rock Country, came seeking evidence to support Hopi migration stories. In his 1895 report, Fewkes wrote: "These rocks had weathered into fantastic shapes suggestive of cathedrals, Greek temples, and sharp steeples of churches extending like giant needles into the sky. . . .This place, I have no doubt, will sooner or later become popular with the sightseer."

Fewkes was also correct about the Hopi connection to Red Rock Country. He gave Hopi names—Palatki and Honanki—to two prehistoric pueblos west of Sedona, though he didn't realize their great age. American archaeology, a relatively new field during Fewkes' time, was only beginning to determine the sequence of human history in the Southwest.

Above: Montezuma Castle.
Opposite: Sinagua ruin at Tuzigoot
National Monument.

From pottery and other lasting materials, later archaeologists developed a picture of Sinaguan culture. Expert agriculturalists, the Sinaguas practiced dry farming, irrigation, and flood-plain agriculture, employing check dams, terraces, and rock-bordered plots (called "waffle gardens") to help catch alluvial soil and protect young plants. They diverted water to earthen reservoirs, some used by ranchers centuries later as stock ponds.

Villagers constructed or replastered pueblos during rainy seasons. Young children helped tend fields of corn, beans, and squash, adding meat of rabbits and other pests to the family stew pot. Men hunted larger game—pronghorn, deer, and elk. Women made plain pottery of reddish clay, including huge storage jars.

Decorated pottery entered the villages via trade. The Sinaguas were "middlemen," surrounded by Ancestral Puebloan, Mogollon, Hohokam, Prescott, and Cohonina territories. Sometime around 1300, near the end of the Southwest's Great Drought, the Sinaguas moved closer to perennial streams, settling in larger hilltop pueblos such as Montezuma Castle and Tuzigoot.

About five thousand Sinaguas lived throughout the area, linked to the north and south by a major trade route. They traded expertly woven cottons and other items for goods from as far away as the Pacific coast and Mexico, including shell jewelry and brightly plumed macaws. Then, little more than a century later, the Sinaguas left their villages behind.

Archaeologists believe that many Sinagua families migrated north, eventually joining other Ancestral Puebloan groups at the Hopi mesas. Others likely stayed behind and intermarried with the Yavapai, returning to hunting and gathering as a way of life.

The mystery, then, is not "where did they go?" but "why?" The Sinaguas had already weathered the Great Drought, and the area's perennial creeks continued to flow. Farmland, game, and wild plants were still plentiful. The Sinaguas appeared to coexist peacefully with the Yavapais, and Athabaskan peoples—the Navajos and Apaches—would not enter the Southwest for another hundred years. It's possible that the desert-dwelling Hohokam people sent raiding parties north after floods destroyed their canals in the late 1300s, but no signs of all-out warfare have been uncovered by archaeologists.

Perhaps, as many Hopi people say, the Sinaguas joined with other Puebloans because it was their shared destiny to live together as Hopituh Shinumu, the peaceful people.

Pool below Wilson Mountain and Ship Rock.

There is something infinitely healing
in the repeated refrains of nature—
the assurance that dawn comes after night,
and spring after the winter.

—RACHEL CARSON

Facing page: The Verde River flows through Dead Horse Ranch State Park.
Left: A Yavapai scout c. 1885.

The Yavapais and Tonto Apaches

Around 1300, when the Sinaguas were moving to large hilltop villages, Yavapai hunter-gatherers entered the Verde Valley. Remnants of Yavapai encampments have been found adjacent to Sinaguan pueblos, suggesting the two cultures traded and lived side by side.

The Tonto Apaches arrived from the northwest as late as A.D. 1500. The Sedona area made a rough territorial boundary between the Yavapais and Tonto Apaches, both semi-nomadic cultures who traveled in bands, or extended family groups. They relied on lightweight tools and built dome-shaped brush shelters where they would stay for a time to hunt or to gather food.

In 1863 Anglo miners discovered gold near Prescott. Farmers, ranchers, and merchants quickly followed, fencing and plowing lands Indians had used seasonally and communally. Conflict was inevitable, and the army established Camp Lincoln (Fort Verde's precursor) in 1865.

After General George Crook took command at Fort Verde in 1871, the army set out after to confine all Yavapais and Apaches to reservations. Many hid in Sedona's red rock canyons, but by 1873, more than two thousand were restricted to a reservation near the Verde River. The Indians were forced to march to the San Carlos Reservation in eastern Arizona in February 1875. Many died on the harsh two-week journey. Conditions at San Carlos, where the Yavapais and Tonto Apaches were incarcerated with rival tribes, were deplorable.

During the next quarter-century, tribes intermarried and adopted Anglo ways. Arizona's population doubled, its wild frontier tamed by railroads, reservoirs, and streets. Many reservation Indians were issued work passes to fill the need for labor. They trickled back to their homeland, but their traditional lifestyles had vanished.

The Yavapais, who still live in the area today, continue to visit ancestral sites like Boynton Canyon, where tribal legend says the first Yavapai man was born.

PIONEERS

SEDONA'S EURO-AMERICAN PIONEERS chose land near Oak Creek, forming three scattered settlements in Oak Creek Canyon, at Red Rock, and at Camp Garden. Clearing land was backbreaking work, done with hand tools and dynamite. Many lived in tent houses before building log or stone cabins, feeding their families by tending gardens and keeping a few chickens or cows.

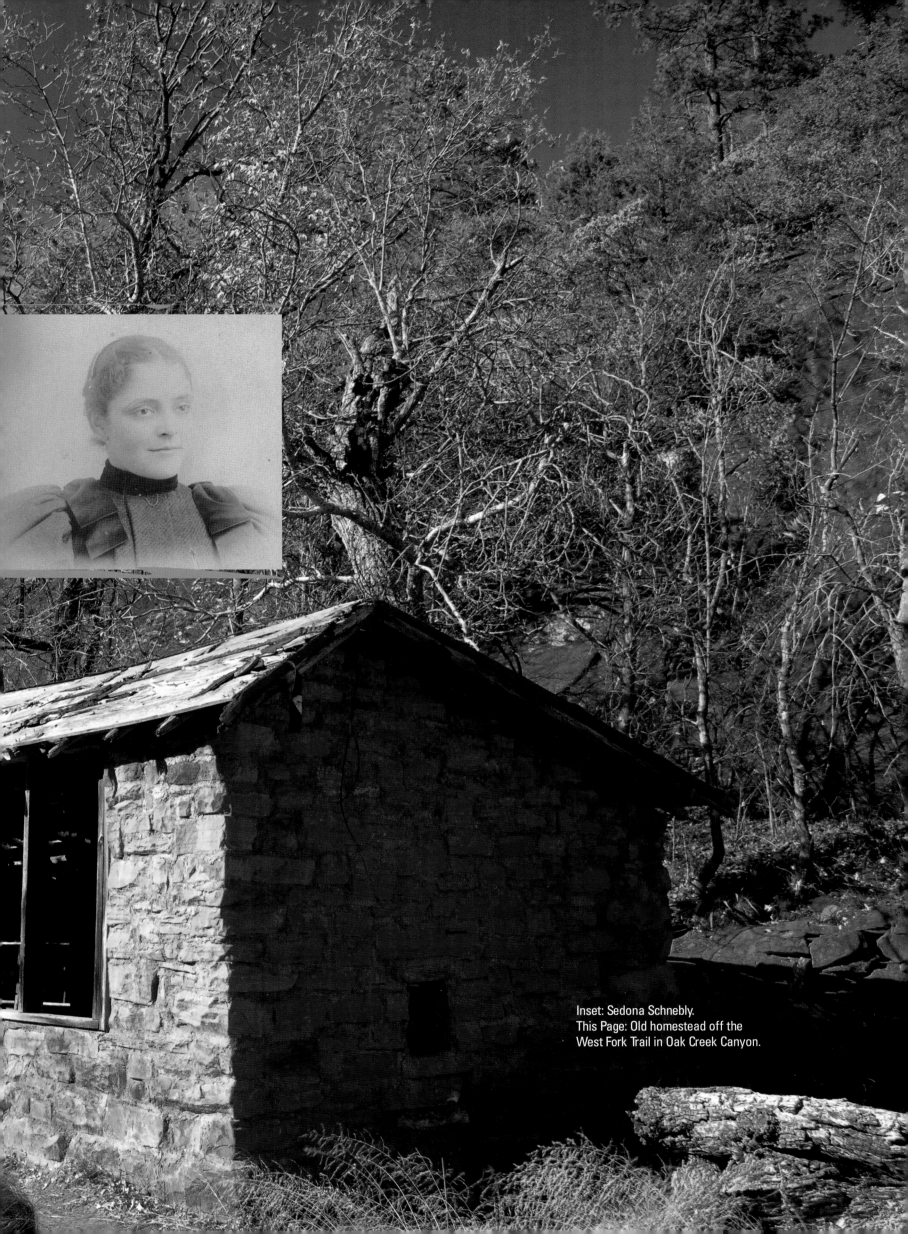

Inset: Sedona Schnebly.
This Page: Old homestead off the
West Fork Trail in Oak Creek Canyon.

Oak Creek Canyon

J. J. Thompson claimed squatter's rights to land in Oak Creek Canyon in 1876 after the Yavapais and Apaches were sent to San Carlos. The previous occupants left behind a vegetable plot, so Thompson named the place Indian Gardens Ranch.

In 1880 C. S. (Jesse) Howard settled about nine miles north, where West Fork enters Oak Creek. The remoteness suited Howard, who was on the run from a jail in California. With him came his daughter and son-in-law, Martha and Steven Purtymun. There was no road up the canyon, so they made a trail down from the Mogollon Rim to the creek to haul belongings and supplies. Howard later sold his place to John "Dad" Thomas, whose sons built cabins nearby.

In 1899 the canyon families established a one-room school midway between the Purtymun and Thompson places. The thirteen students in the log cabin school included six Thompsons, six Purtymuns, and one Thomas. Clara Purtymun recalled walking three miles to school, crossing the creek several times to get there, often to discover on the way home that bear tracks had covered over the children's earlier footprints.

Red Rock

The same year that Thompson claimed Indian Gardens Ranch, a man named John Lee settled along Oak Creek several miles downstream. In 1884 Henry and Dorette Schuerman moved to a 160-acre parcel that Henry had gotten in exchange for a $500 debt. As othzers settled nearby, including the Dumas and Armijo families, this area became known as Red Rock. By 1891 there were enough children in the Red Rock neighborhood to establish the first area school.

Opposite: Oak Creek during a light monsoon rain.
Above: Oak Creek tumbles over rocks at Allen's Bend.

Opposite: West Fork of Oak Creek.
Left and Above: Old homestead, J.J. Thompson family.
Below left: Abraham James family (top) and the Schuermans (bottom).

Camp Garden

Between Red Rock and Oak Creek Canyon, a shaded creek crossing had become a favorite fishing retreat for soldiers from Fort Verde. The soldiers nicknamed the spot Camp Garden. The first to settle land in this area was Abraham James, who brought his family here in 1879 at Jim Thompson's suggestion. Abraham's daughter Margaret married Thompson in 1880, and their son Frank was the first white child born in the area.

The first to "prove up" or patent land here was the Owenby family, whose homestead was at the present-day site of Los Abrigados resort. In 1901 Frank Owenby sold his land to a young couple from Missouri named Schnebly. They had heard about the area's beauty and climate from Mr. Schnebly's brother Ellsworth, who taught at the Oak Creek Canyon school. The Schneblys soon built a two-story frame house along the creek.

T. C. "Carl" Schnebly and others saw the need for mail service, and in 1902 he applied to the government for a post office. He suggested the names "Oak Creek Crossing," then "Schnebly Station," but regulations at that time required new post offices to have a cancellation stamp with a single word. Ellsworth suggested that Carl use his wife's name, and so the growing community became known as "Sedona."

Surrounding land had been established as a forest preserve in 1899, and in 1905 a forest ranger was assigned to the area. Early ranger duties included counting the cattle and sheep grazing on forest ranges. The route used to transport livestock to summer pastures was the Munds trail. Many travelers stayed at the Schnebly home at the foot of the trail to break the journey, and the route became known as Schnebly Hill Road.

Historic Sedona

By 1912 four Sedona families had enough children to start a school. It was located on Brewer Road, and forest ranger Claude Thompson's wife became the schoolteacher. A ranger station was built across the road in 1917. Sedona families dug irrigation ditches to their properties, raising fruit and vegetables and grazing small herds, selling what they didn't need in the bustling mining and lumber towns of Jerome and Flagstaff.

Homesteading in Sedona continued into the 1930s. W. A. Jordan was one of several Verde Valley farmers whose crops had been destroyed by fumes from copper smelters near Jerome. He relocated to Sedona, and his sons George and Walter followed, raising strawberries, vegetables, apples, and peaches.

When the Great Depression arrived, Sedona's farmers formed a cooperative, delivering their produce to the Jordan packing shed. Sedona-grown produce traveled to Flagstaff, Phoenix, and even San Francisco.

The Depression hit cities hardest, and young men who joined the Civilian Conservation Corps (CCC) were sent to rural areas for work. By the late 1930s, the CCC housed two to three hundred young men in barracks near the old James property. CCC crews fought forest fires, planted trees, constructed roads, and strung cattle fences. They built the forest service barn and helped install a water system for the ranger station and school.

Left: Schnebly home.
Above: Munds Mountain Wilderness near Sedona.

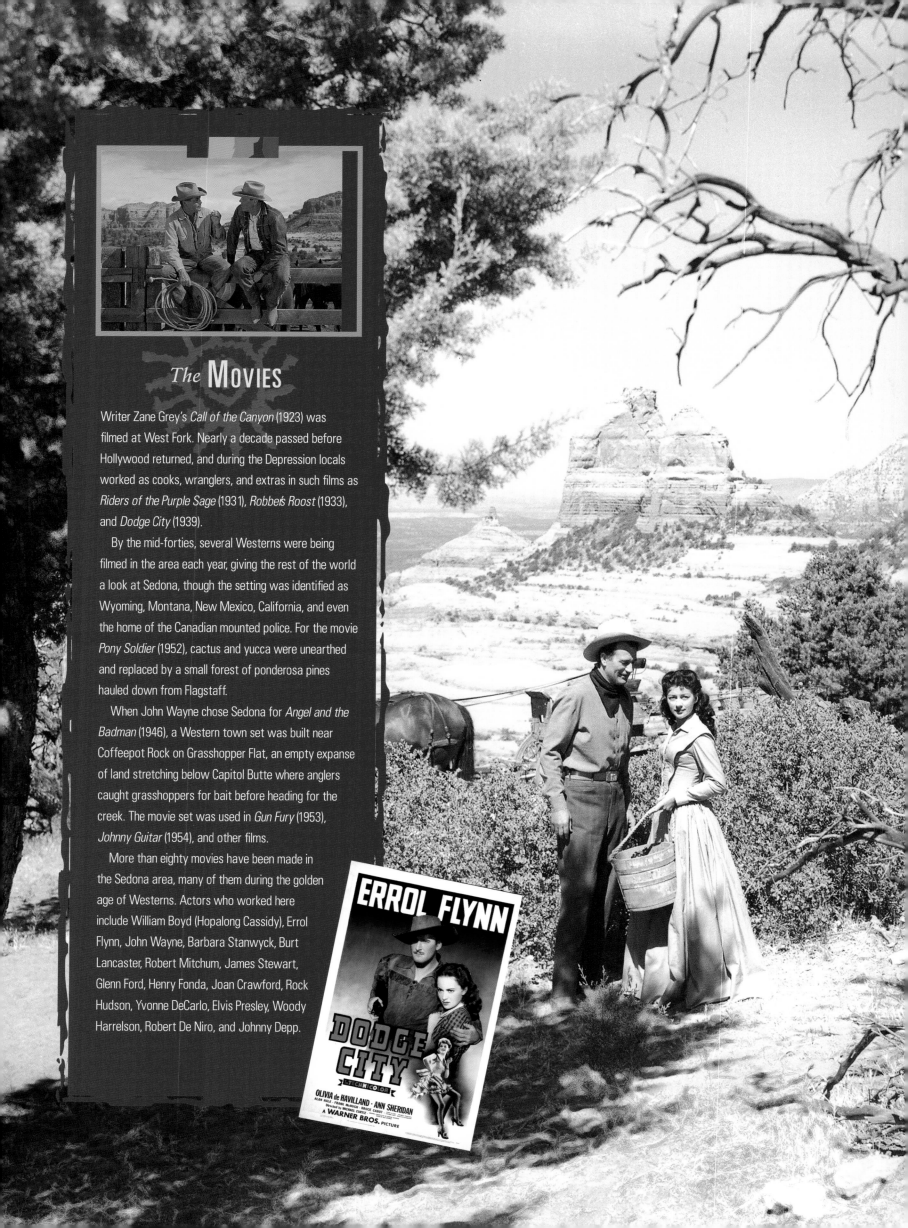

The MOVIES

Writer Zane Grey's *Call of the Canyon* (1923) was filmed at West Fork. Nearly a decade passed before Hollywood returned, and during the Depression locals worked as cooks, wranglers, and extras in such films as *Riders of the Purple Sage* (1931), *Robber's Roost* (1933), and *Dodge City* (1939).

By the mid-forties, several Westerns were being filmed in the area each year, giving the rest of the world a look at Sedona, though the setting was identified as Wyoming, Montana, New Mexico, California, and even the home of the Canadian mounted police. For the movie *Pony Soldier* (1952), cactus and yucca were unearthed and replaced by a small forest of ponderosa pines hauled down from Flagstaff.

When John Wayne chose Sedona for *Angel and the Badman* (1946), a Western town set was built near Coffeepot Rock on Grasshopper Flat, an empty expanse of land stretching below Capitol Butte where anglers caught grasshoppers for bait before heading for the creek. The movie set was used in *Gun Fury* (1953), *Johnny Guitar* (1954), and other films.

More than eighty movies have been made in the Sedona area, many of them during the golden age of Westerns. Actors who worked here include William Boyd (Hopalong Cassidy), Errol Flynn, John Wayne, Barbara Stanwyck, Burt Lancaster, Robert Mitchum, James Stewart, Glenn Ford, Henry Fonda, Joan Crawford, Rock Hudson, Yvonne DeCarlo, Elvis Presley, Woody Harrelson, Robert De Niro, and Johnny Depp.

West Sedona

In 1948 the first well was dug in Grasshopper Flat, and development was no longer limited to the environs of Oak Creek. The former movie set eventually made way for Sedona West, one of the town's first subdivisions, with street names commemorating film titles. Today, Grasshopper Flat is the main residential and service area known as West Sedona.

The Village of Oak Creek

A dirt road (now State Route 179) led south to the old Beaverhead Stage station and, by the 1930s, to a few small homesteads that practiced dry farming. There were no wells in this wide-open area called Big Park. Farmers and ranchers used earthen tanks to capture runoff or hauled water from Oak Creek. Big Park's Bell Rock and Courthouse Butte made a dramatic backdrop for several films, including *The Rounders* (1965).

During the 1940s, Fannie Belle Gulick, a Las Vegas woman (whose "boardinghouse for miners" may have actually been a bordello), began acquiring land in Big Park and Grasshopper Flat. She hired well-driller Carl Williams, who went on to drill fifty wells in the Sedona area, making residential growth possible.

After Gulick's death, developers purchased her land in Big Park and designed a golf course and resort known as the Village of Oakcreek (spelled Oak Creek today). Oakcreek Country Club opened in 1968, shortly after the Poco Diablo golf course opened a few miles to the north.

Following the canyon retreats of the twenties and thirties, and the roadside motels of the forties and fifties, golf resorts and spas turned a new page in the town's history of hospitality. You could say that Sedona Schnebly started it all, opening her door to travelers as the century began.

From Apples to Art

Western films introduced audiences to Sedona's fabulous scenery, and after World War II, more people began visiting and relocating to the red rocks. Among the newcomers were film people and artists. In 1946 Max Ernst, who influenced Europe's Surrealist movement, settled along Brewer Road. He returned to Paris in 1953, renting his house to Nassan Gobran, an Egyptian sculptor who'd come to Sedona to teach at the fledgling Verde Valley School. Hamilton Warren had founded the private boarding school in the Big Park area in the late 1940s and contacted Gobran to launch the school's art department.

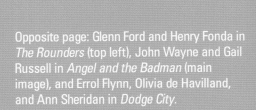

Opposite page: Glenn Ford and Henry Fonda in *The Rounders* (top left), John Wayne and Gail Russell in *Angel and the Badman* (main image), and Errol Flynn, Olivia de Havilland, and Ann Sheridan in *Dodge City*.

Right: Apple orchard near Slide Rock.

Gobran quit working at the school to teach summer art classes, which evolved into the Sedona Arts Center (SAC). SAC found a home in George Jordan's old apple-packing barn in 1958, and for many decades, the barn was the hub of Sedona's social life, with classes, concerts, plays, dinners, costume parties, and of course, art shows. SAC continues to host exhibits and classes in a new building that opened adjacent to the old barn in 1994.

In 1965 a group of Western painters—including Sedona's Joe Beeler—founded the Cowboy Artists of America while tipping a few at the Oak Creek Tavern. They hoped to "perpetuate the memory and culture of the Old West." In Sedona, ranches and orchards were giving way to housing development, with lots in West Sedona selling for $2,500. A few historic structures still stand in Uptown, including the former home of the Jordan family. One of the finest examples of red rock territorial architecture, it's now a museum operated by the Sedona Historical Society, with exhibits on homesteading, ranching, and moviemaking.

In 1971 developer Abe Miller began constructing a Spanish colonial–style arts village along the creek. Tlaquepaque was completed in 1978, after years of careful craftsmanship, its stairways curving around sycamores in order to preserve the site's natural beauty. Tlaquepaque's centuries-old ambiance anchors this section of State Route 179, currently home to numerous art galleries.

Monthly gallery tours stretch from Hillside to Uptown, and cultural events—from the venerable Jazz on the Rocks to the Plein Air Festival—have established Sedona's reputation as an art town. Frequently recognized as one of the top art destinations in the U.S., Sedona continues to inspire artists and visitors alike.

Above left: "Red Rock Pass," oil painting by Bill Cramer.
Above: Tlaquepaque lit by luminarias.

Exploring
Red Rock Country

National Forest, wilderness areas, and state parks offer a half-dozen public campgrounds, several picnic areas, and scores of hiking trails, all inviting a deeper experience with this magical landscape. You can soar over Sedona in a plane, helicopter, or hot air balloon; go on a guided hike; or take a wheeled excursion on almost anything from mountain bike to trolley.

The moon rises over the red cliffs of Sedona.
Inset: Petoglyph of a human with staff.

Scenic Drives

Sedona's first designated scenic route, State Route 89A through Oak Creek Canyon, begins north of Uptown and ascends Oak Creek Canyon for twelve miles, passing charming lodges, Slide Rock State Park, and forest service sites for camping, picnicking, swimming, or fishing. A dozen hiking trails follow the creek or climb the canyon's craggy walls, including the wildly popular West Fork Trail, which begins at Call of the Canyon.

Voted one of America's ten best road trips, the scenic Red Rock Byway (State Route 179) leads from Uptown to the Village of Oak Creek. The scenery continues beyond Interstate I-17: The highway becomes Forest Road (FR) 618, a good gravel road that passes over Beaver Creek and leads to the V-Bar-V Ranch Heritage Site. Here, a cliff face displays Sinaguan petroglyphs dating between A.D. 1150 and 1400.

West of Sedona, Red Rock Loop Road (FR 216) descends from the high school toward Oak Creek, offering spectacular vistas of Cathedral Rock. Head for popular Crescent Moon Ranch to swim, picnic, hike, or capture one of Arizona's most-photographed views on camera.

Across the creek from Tlaquepaque, Schnebly Hill Road (FR 153) is a rough-and-rocky but popular scenic drive, winding around Technicolor Corner and climbing to the Cowpies and Merry-Go-Round Rock. For the same views and a richer experience, take a guided jeep tour or hike up the Munds Wagon Trail.

You can make a loop of the paved and dirt roads around Boynton Pass to hike Doe Mesa or other trails, or to see prehistoric cliff dwellings and rock art. Reservations are recommended for Palatki, located northwest of Sedona at the end of FR 795. Honanki is four miles farther on rocky FR 525. Sinagua villagers occupied these pueblos around A.D. 1150.

Oak Creek offers a wealth of recreation, from scenic drives and quiet hikes (below) to the thrill of sliding down the slick surface of Slide Rock (opposite).

Trails

More than three hundred miles of trails, many accessible within Sedona's city limits, lead into the 1.8-million-acre Coconino National Forest. Popular hikes include shady West Fork, panoramic Doe Mesa, and mystical Boynton Canyon. Several hub trailheads, including ones on Jordan and Schnebly Hill roads, offer parking for equestrians. Backpackers and experienced hikers can head down bumpy forest roads to find solitude and longer routes, such as the Secret Canyon or Loy Canyon trails.

Though mountain biking is prohibited in Sedona's designated wilderness areas, singletrack enthusiasts will find technical challenges on Cathedral Loop, Chicken Point, and other trails. Bell Rock Pathway, Big Park Loop, and several forest roads are good choices for beginners and families. Head to a local bike shop to rent equipment or join a guided ride, or to a forest service visitor center for trail maps and information.

Above: A rainbow follows a storm above Coffeepot Rock.
Opposite: The last light of day makes Cathedral Rock glow at Red Rock Crossing.

SPIRIT *of* SEDONA

One of Sedona's most inspiring landmarks, the Chapel of the Holy Cross, was completed in 1956. The central feature of Marguerite Brunswig Staude's contemporary design is a reinforced steel cross that rises nearly a hundred feet out of the rock below.

Stunning views from the chapel's walkway incorporate Bell Rock and Cathedral Rock, both formations identified by a local psychic in 1980 as locations that amplified or focused particular types of energy emanating from the earth. The New Age movement soared in the 1980s, as more psychics and writers described Sedona's vortex sites, and the 1987 Harmonic Convergence attracted throngs to the sandstone slopes of Bell Rock.

Often attributed to the New Age, theories about earth energy are ages-old. Geomancy, whether you think of it as earth magic or simply a response to the environment, has been important to all cultures through time. Yavapai tribal members identify Bell Rock as the place where cultural hero and shaman Skatakaamcha destroyed a predatory monster.

Believers and skeptics can agree on one thing: Sedona's deepest magic is the way the red rocks awaken us to the enduring majesty and mystery of Earth.

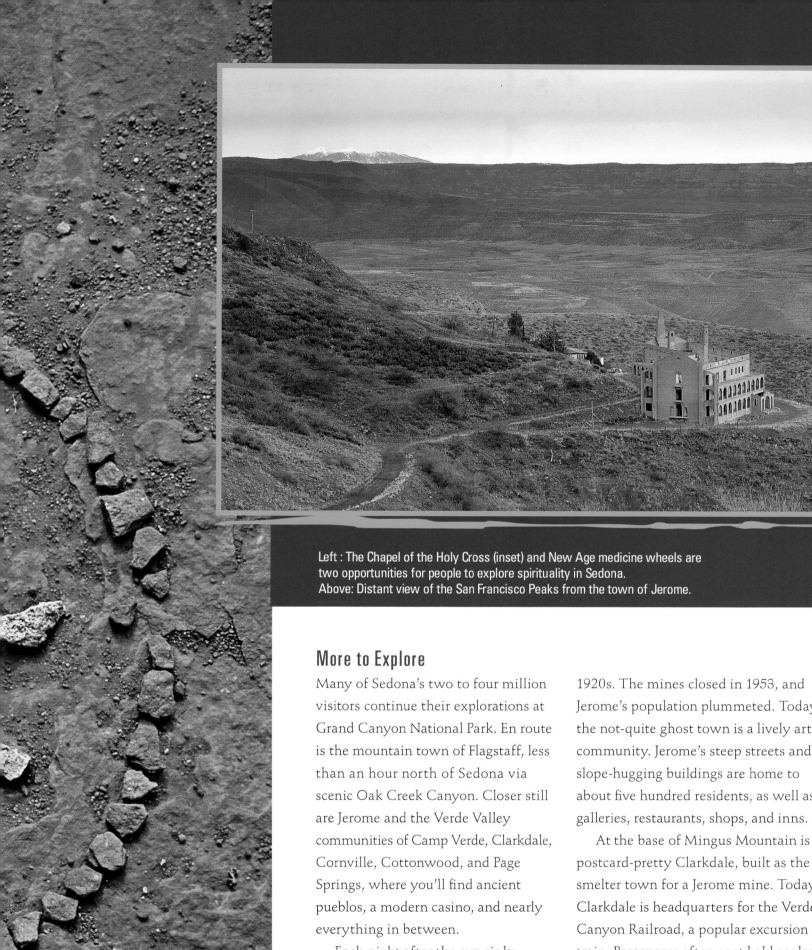

Left : The Chapel of the Holy Cross (inset) and New Age medicine wheels are two opportunities for people to explore spirituality in Sedona.
Above: Distant view of the San Francisco Peaks from the town of Jerome.

More to Explore

Many of Sedona's two to four million visitors continue their explorations at Grand Canyon National Park. En route is the mountain town of Flagstaff, less than an hour north of Sedona via scenic Oak Creek Canyon. Closer still are Jerome and the Verde Valley communities of Camp Verde, Clarkdale, Cornville, Cottonwood, and Page Springs, where you'll find ancient pueblos, a modern casino, and nearly everything in between.

Each night after the sun sinks behind Mingus Mountain, the lights of Jerome twinkle enticingly. When Sedona was an agricultural community of a few families, Jerome, once known as "the wickedest town in the West," was a mining boomtown with a population that peaked at fifteen thousand in the

1920s. The mines closed in 1953, and Jerome's population plummeted. Today the not-quite ghost town is a lively arts community. Jerome's steep streets and slope-hugging buildings are home to about five hundred residents, as well as galleries, restaurants, shops, and inns.

At the base of Mingus Mountain is postcard-pretty Clarkdale, built as the smelter town for a Jerome mine. Today Clarkdale is headquarters for the Verde Canyon Railroad, a popular excursion train. Passengers often spot bald eagles and other wildlife on the half-day trip, billed as "Arizona's longest-running nature show." The route cuts through a steep-walled section of Verde Canyon and edges remote Sycamore Canyon, with its colorful Redwall Limestone and Supai cliffs.

Top: Montezuma Well, part of
Montezuma Castle National Monument.
Above: Historic Fort Verde.

Southeast of Clarkdale, a prehistoric Sinaguan village named Tuzigoot (Apache for "crooked water") perches on a hilltop overlooking the Verde River. Artifacts and displays highlight the Sinagua culture's golden age, when large pueblos like Tuzigoot dotted the Verde River's curving path through the valley.

A tributary, Beaver Creek, links two other fascinating prehistoric sites administered by the National Park Service. Montezuma Castle, a multistory cliff-dwelling, sheltered Sinaguans during their last decades in the Verde Valley. Six miles away is Montezuma Well, a limestone sinkhole. Prehistoric farmers diverted the well's natural outlet to water their fields. Their canals, hardened by the mineral-laden water, can still be seen a thousand years later.

The first area community to be settled by Anglo farmers and ranchers was Camp Verde. In 1865 soldiers erected a tent camp at West Clear Creek to protect settlers from Indian raids. Fort Verde moved to its present site in 1871. History comes to life when costumed reenactors portray cavalry officers and their wives, showing off their riding skills, or demonstrating gentler arts like lace-making. In December, the fort celebrates a Victorian Christmas. Other festivals, such as February's pecan festival and the Cornfest in July, recall Camp Verde's rural roots.

Southwest of Sedona, Oak Creek waters the farms and vineyards of Cornville and Page Springs. Wineries host tours and tastings, and orchards offer fresh peaches, pomegranates, apples, and other seasonal fruits. Anglers can try their luck at the Page Springs fish hatchery, also a birdwatcher's delight because of the many species attracted to its cottonwood-lined creekside.

Though Cottonwood is the modern shopping and service hub for Verde Valley residents, its Old Town has a historic flavor, with stone buildings, antique shops, and the Jail Trail, leading to the Verde River Greenway State Natural Area and Dead Horse Ranch State Park. Each April, the park hosts the "Birdy Verde," a can't-miss festival for birders. In September, Verde River Days celebrates Arizona's only designated wild and scenic river.

Whether you picture yourself staying in a luxurious spa or pitching a cliff-edge camp, seeking the Wild West or wildflowers, you'll find unmatched variety and amazing vistas in Sedona and the Verde Valley.

Red Rock bluffs in Coconino National Forest
near Sedona.

And this, our life, exempt from public haunt,

finds tongues in trees, books in the running brooks,

sermons in stones, and good in everything.

—WILLIAM SHAKESPEARE